*A Soul Journey Through the Chambers of the Self*
*Shamanic Series: Book I*

By Mindi Staley

ISBN: 979-8-9999946-0-8

Choose Your Own Awakening: A Soul Journey Through the
Chambers of the Self
Shamanic Series: Book I
First Edition

Cover and interior design by the author
Printed in the United States of America

This book is an inspirational spark of creativity. While
inspired by the author's lived experiences, it is presented as a
symbolic and spiritual guide. It is not intended as medical,
psychological, or therapeutic advice. Readers are encouraged
to seek professional support where needed.

## Dedication

For the ones who question if healing is possible.

For the ones who keep breathing when it seems easier to stop.

For the inner children, the future elders, and the angels who remember.

This is for you.

## Acknowledgments

To every teacher, healer, guide, and beloved who held a lantern as I stumbled through the dark — thank you.

To the medicine keepers, the sacred lands, and the unseen allies who reminded me of the wisdom in the breath and the holiness of the path — this book carries your essence.

To friends who witnessed me — messy, luminous, and in-between — thank you.

To the women I've sat in circle with, bared my soul with, and remembered alongside — you are woven into every chapter.

To my family of origin — my grandparents, my mother, my father, my sisters, my niece & nephew, my cousins, aunts, and uncles — thank you for sharing in the heart that created this.

And to the magical soul family I've remembered along the way: we are all students and teachers for one another. Mirrors and reflections, ever "walking each other home" (Ram Dass).

And to you, dear reader — for your trust, your courage, your choosing. You make this living prayer real.

## Preface

This book was born from the ashes, breath, and joy of my own becoming. It carries echoes of pain I once silenced, wisdom I once forgot, and light I finally let shine through me.

Its roots stretch into two places within me. First, into the adventure books I enjoyed as a child — stories that gave me agency, possibility, and escape during traumatic times. And second, into the shamanic energy medicine path I now walk — not as something entirely new, but as a remembering of the gifts that have always lived inside me.

These threads — the child who longed for paths and choices, and the woman who reawakened her medicine — weave together here. This is both a book and a ceremony, a story and a mirror. It does not tell you who you are- it sits beside you as you remember.

This foundational book of the series offers glimpses into shamanic wisdom. Chambers of the soul retrieval journey, spirit animals, and a labyrinth of choices. It is a spiral, not a straight line. You may return again and again, discovering more of the magical wonder that is your soul.

May these pages meet you wherever you are — whether standing at the threshold, dancing through the fire, or returning home to the temple within.

With Love & Gratitude,
Mindi

## Foreword

Welcome, beloved traveler.

You did not stumble upon this book. It called you — softly, curiously, or perhaps with the thunder of inevitability.

This is not a traditional story. It is a map of many paths. A living mirror. An invitation back to your Self.

Here, you will not be told how to heal, learn, or explore. Instead, you'll be offered choices — reflections to notice, patterns to recognize, and opportunities to transform.

The invitation is to enter this experience gently, knowing at all times you are the creator. You are safe. You may laugh, you may cry. Some pages may stir old memories — tender or jagged. Others may feel like prophecies. None of this is a mistake. What rises is not here to harm you, but to be witnessed, honored, and perhaps even gently let go.

The Ritual Invitations at the start of each chapter are here to support you — before, during, and after. They are practices you can return to whenever the path feels heavy or unclear.

There are no wrong turns, only sacred detours. No 'right' way through. Only your way. And it is perfect.

Each chapter is a door. Each path you choose belongs to you — guiding you deeper into remembrance.

So breathe deep. Turn the page. And choose your own awakening.

# Table of Contents

# Chapter 1: The Fog Rolls In

Before remembering comes forgetting. Every soul that enters this life passes through the veil — a sacred fog that blurs the brilliance of our origin. It is not punishment, but protection. To walk as humans, we must first forget the fullness of who we are. Only then can the journey of remembering begin.

**Opening Portal: Ritual Invitation**

Breathe into your belly and connect to your body. Begin here, in the mist. Connect to the mystery of not-knowing. The fog is not against you — it is with you.

Consider one or more of the following ritual invitations to ground and open:

• Fog Dance — Step into imaginary mist as if it were music. Sway slowly as though the fog itself were your partner. Let your body remember the joy of not knowing where the next step will land.

• Soul Map — Free-write from the prompt: "When I feel lost, I…"

• Mist Mirror — Gaze at your reflection until your features blur. Whisper: "I am still here."

These rituals may return anytime clarity feels far away.

## Scene One: The Veil Lowers

The fog arrives like a secret keeper. It slips between you and your own reflection, drapes itself across your memories, and quiets the bright pulse of your essence.

You do not resist — you cannot. The veil is part of the passage. It enfolds you, tender and relentless, softening every edge until even your own name feels far away.

Inside the mist, time bends. You are no longer before, not yet after. You are suspended — between worlds, between selves.

And still, something stirs. A faint awareness beneath the haze. The pulse of a truth you cannot see but somehow still know. The soul whispers through the fog:

I remain.

It is not clarity you are given now, but concealment. Not direction, but pause. The forgetting holds you, asking only this: Will you linger here long enough to feel what has been veiled?

### A Sacred Invitation to Choose Your Path

Drift — Keep moving through the haze. Let the fog carry you, silent and unseen. → Go to Scene Two A on page 9

Greve — Feel the emptiness inside the mist. Touch the grief of your own vanishing. → Go to Scene Two B on page 10

Play — Laugh in the unknowing. Relate to forgetting as part of the cosmic game. → Go to Scene Two C on page 11

## Scene Two A: The Sleepwalker

You adapt to the fog as though it is normal.

You keep the motions moving.

Wake. Work. Speak. Smile. Sleep.

The days blur together like a watercolor washed too many times.

Nothing is sharp enough to hurt — or to hold.

And yet, deep in your belly, there is a restlessness.

The fog is heavy.

The body knows this weight is not meant to last forever.

You have survived. But you have not fully lived.

If you lose yourself in the mist, go to Path A at the end of this chapter, or…

If you're ready to see more clearly, turn to Chapter 9: The Reckoning of Projection on page 61,

Or perhaps…

You glimpse your own reflection — but the eyes are those of a wolf. If you follow the wolf… leap to Chapter 6: The Dance of Narcissus on page 37.

## Scene Two B: The Vanished

You feel the sting of perceived disconnection. The grief of your own disappearing act. You don't run from it this time. You let the tears come.

Or the numbness.

Or nothing at all.

You place your hand over your chest. And say to yourself: *I miss you.*

Something shifts. Not in the world — but in you.

You heard the ache. You didn't abandon it. And that... is holy.

If you're ready to honor this ache toward healing, go to Path B at the end of this chapter, or...

If you long to explore how disconnection formed in your earliest bonds, turn to Chapter 3: The Allure of Escape on page 19,

Or perhaps...

A memory returns: a hummingbird hovering just outside your childhood window. If you follow the flutter... leap to Chapter 7: The Mirror Break on page 45.

## Scene Two C: The Joyful One

You play within the fog, letting it swirl around you.

You giggle at how quickly things can be forgotten — and how just as quickly they return. You twirl in the mist, sensing that even this forgetting is part of the dance.

The fog doesn't only conceal; it teases and reveals.

It hides the obvious only to offer it back again — brighter, lighter, somehow more alive.

This is not exile but play — a cosmic hide-and-seek where the soul delights in losing and finding itself.

If you celebrate the laughter, go to Path C at the end of this chapter, or…

If play awakens your trickster spirit, turn to Chapter 7: The Mirror Break on page 45,

Or perhaps…

You dream of a box of photographs sinking into a river. One floats back up, soaked but glowing. If you reach for it… leap to Chapter 10: The Chamber of Wounds on page 67.

# Chapter 1: Paths A, B, & C

---

**Path A** — You drifted with the mist, letting it carry you through. This is not wrong. This is survival. But the body remembers the weight. The soul remembers the light. And they will call you home again.

From here, you may continue directly forward into Chapter 2: The Masked Beginning

---

**Path B** — You honored the emptiness. You let yourself feel. You stayed present with the one who was left behind. Even in the haze, you found the faint outline of your own heart. You are already remembering. You are reuniting with your Self. And that changes everything.

From here, you may continue directly forward into Chapter 2: The Masked Beginning

---

**Path C** — You danced with the fog and called forgetting part of the game. This is not a mistake. It is the cosmic joke: the soul hiding from itself only to be found again. The fog teaches through laughter and surprise — revealing what was hidden in plain sight. You are playing. You are alive.

From here, you may continue directly forward into Chapter 2: The Masked Beginning

# Chapter 2: The Masked Beginning

You arrive at the first shaping — where identity grows not from truth, but from necessity. Here, the soul learns its first disguise, believing it must perform to be loved.

### Opening Portal: Ritual Invitation

Breathe into your belly and connect to your body. Let the mask be held with compassion, not shame.
Consider one or more of the following ritual invitations to ground and open:

• Self-Portrait — Draw or describe your 'public' self and your 'private' self. Where do they align or diverge?

• Breath Reveal — Inhale deeply and exhale with sound. Let go of the performance, just for a breath.

• Mask Meditation — Close your eyes and imagine removing a mask from your face. Ask: Who am I beneath this?

These rituals may return whenever you forget who you are beneath the performance.

## Scene One: The Mask Forms

It was subtle.
No one told you to hide.
But the world rewarded the version of you that smiled.
That performed.
That got it right.

You learned quickly.
When I am this — they stay.
When I am that — they pull away.

And so, the mask was born.

Charming. Achieving. Pleasing.
Empathic. Adaptable. Good.

It fit so well, you forgot it was there.
You called it personality.
You called it identity.

But your body always knew.

The fatigue from over-smiling.
The tension from over-agreeing.
The ache from never quite being seen.

The mask kept you safe.
But it also kept you separate.

Until now.

**A Sacred Invitation to Choose Your Path**

Keep Wearing It — Safety over truth. → Go to Scene Two A on page 15

Peek Beneath — Risk a glimpse of the real you. → Go to Scene Two B on page 16

Remove It Entirely — Leap into full exposure. → Go to Scene Two C on page 16

---

## Scene Two A: The Loyal Mask

You keep smiling.
Keep performing.
You say what they want to hear — and it works.

But the cost is quiet... and growing.

Your body aches for the breath that comes with being real.

If you stay within the experience of self-protection, go to Path A at the end of this chapter, or...

If safety has replaced authenticity, turn to Chapter 14: The Reclaiming on page 95,

Or perhaps...

You see your reflection crack — and behind it, another face entirely. If you are curious about it, leap to Chapter 6: The Dance of Narcissus on page 37.

## Scene Two B: The Risk Taker

You lift the mask just enough for air touch your skin.
Someone might see you.
It's terrifying.
It's alive.

The relief in your chest tells you — this is the way forward.

If you stay within the experience of tentative truth, go to Path B at the end of this chapter, or…

If you're ready to breathe without the mask, turn to Chapter 5: The Disappearing Act on page 31,

Or perhaps…

A hand offers you a different mask — one you've never worn. If you take it, leap to Chapter 11: The Chamber of Contracts on page 75.

## Scene Two C: The Unmasker

You drop the mask completely.
The air feels strange on your skin.
You're too visible.
And yet — you're breathing fully for the first time in years.

If you stay within the experience of radical authenticity, go to Path C at the end of this chapter, or…

If full exposure scares you but excites you, turn to Chapter 10: The Chamber of Wounds on page 67,

Or perhaps…

You laugh so hard the mask dissolves in your hands. If you feel lighter, leap to Chapter 9: The Reckoning of Projection on page 61.

# Chapter 2: Paths A, B, & C

---

**Path A** — You stayed behind the mask. It's familiar. It feels safer. But your shoulders ache from carrying the weight, and your jaw tightens with every word unspoken. You know this costume well — it has earned you belonging. Yet beneath it, the soul presses against the fabric, longing for air, longing for light. The truth will call again.

From here, you may continue directly forward into Chapter 3: The Allure of Escape

---

**Path B** — You dared to peek beneath. Just for a moment, you let the mask slip. A shiver ran through your chest. Your breath deepened. It may not seem like much — but this is the way authenticity begins: as a seed planted in soil.

From here, you may continue directly forward into Chapter 3: The Allure of Escape

---

**Path C** — You revealed yourself fully. No filter. No disguise. Your heart naked, your voice trembling but true. It feels both terrifying and liberating — like stepping into open air after years underground. Every nerve hums with aliveness. Your body remembers what freedom feels like. Vulnerability is courage — it is proof that you are alive, awake, and real.

From here, you may continue directly forward into Chapter 3: The Allure of Escape

# Chapter 3: The Allure of Escape

Here lies the soft temptation of escape mechanisms — doorways that promise relief, distraction, numbing…a pause from the ache. You've walked through these before, maybe without even noticing. But this chapter asks: what if you stayed instead of slipping away?

**Opening Portal: Ritual Invitation**

Breathe into your belly and connect to your body. Allow the part of you that longs to escape to be met with compassion. Consider one or more of the following ritual invitations to ground and open:

• Cloud Gaze — Lay down and watch the sky. Let your mind wander, then gently call it home to your body.

• Pulse Check — Pause and place your fingers on your wrist. Feel your pulse. Whisper, "I am still here."

• Honest Reflection — Write: "What I reach for when I don't want to feel is…" and follow it without judgment.

These rituals may return when escape calls louder than presence.

## Scene One: The Big Escape

It starts with a twitch.
A flick of the thumb.
A scroll, a sip, a snack.

Just a little escape.

Just a moment of relief.
Just something to take the edge off.

The noise inside you feels too loud.
The ache too ancient.
The discomfort too much.

So you vanish — not in body, but in presence.
You're still here... but not really.

Your eyes glaze.
Your breath flattens.
Your body keeps going while your soul takes a break.

And it works.
Until it doesn't.

Because after the glass is empty, the feed is stale, the binge is done...
you're still here.

Still aching.
Still untouched.
Still longing for something real.

You remember that you can't escape what's inside you.
But you *can* choose to meet it differently.

**A Sacred Invitation to Choose Your Path**

Walk Away Again — Choose the comfort of avoidance. →
Go to Scene Two A on page 21

Stay Present — Feel what's here without running. → Go to Scene Two B on page 22

See the Pattern — Notice when escape becomes the habit. → Go to Scene Two C on page 23

---

## Scene Two A: The Avoider

You choose the show, the drink, the scroll.
It's easier than the ache.
And for now — it works.

But somewhere inside, you know: you're postponing a meeting that will change everything.

If you stay within the experience of postponement, go to Path A at the end of this chapter, or...

If avoidance feels safer than truth, turn to Chapter 10: The Chamber of Wounds on page 67,

Or perhaps...

You dream of running down a hallway with no doors. Suddenly, one appears. If you open it... leap to Chapter 12: The Chamber of Grace on page 81.

## Scene Two B: The Stayer

You close the app.
Put down the glass.
And breathe.

At first, the discomfort blooms sharp and insistent —a knot in your stomach, a buzzing in your chest, a heat rising in your throat.

But you stay.
Your feet press into the ground.
Your breath widens in your ribs.

And then, something shifts.
You feel more here.
More real.
Even in the ache.

Presence hurts at first — but then it begins to feel like home.

If you stay within the experience of grounded presence, go to Path B at the end of this chapter, or…

If you're ready to explore what the ache is guarding, turn to Chapter 5: The Disappearing Act on page 31,

Or perhaps…

A small bird lands on your knee. If you ask what it's here to teach you, leap to Chapter 13: The Chamber of Treasures on page 89.

---

## Scene Two C: The Witness

You start to notice. The way your hand twitches toward the phone. The way your mind drifts just before the ache arrives. The way your body leans toward escape without asking permission.

But this time, you don't judge it. You simply see it. And in the seeing, something loosens. The habit loses a little of its grip. A small gap opens between impulse and action — a doorway you didn't know you had.

This is the gift of awareness: it doesn't end the habit, but it breaks the spell.

If you stay within the experience of self-observation, go to Path C at the end of this chapter, or...

If you're ready to see the roots of the habit, turn to Chapter 11: The Chamber of Contracts on page 75,

Or perhaps...

You find a half-finished puzzle on the table. If you sit down to finish it, leap to Chapter 9: The Reckoning of Projection on page 61.

# Chapter 3: Paths A, B, & C

**Path A** — You chose the escape. You left yourself again. It's okay — this is how you've survived. Relief was chosen over presence.

But the ache will return, carrying the same invitation.

From here, you may continue directly forward into Chapter 4: The Voice That Vanished

**Path B** — You stayed present. You breathed through the burn of discomfort. Your body remembered what it feels like to hold both ache and aliveness in the same space. This is courage — not grand or flashy, but steady.

And it changes everything.

From here, you may continue directly forward into Chapter 4: The Voice That Vanished

**Path C** — You witnessed the pattern. You saw the habit forming in real time, and in that seeing, something loosened.

Awareness became a doorway to freedom. You stepped through it — not to escape, but to return, gently, to yourself.

From here, you may continue directly forward into Chapter 4: The Voice That Vanished

# Chapter 4: The Voice That Vanished

There was a time when your voice moved without hesitation — when truth leapt from your tongue before fear could catch it. Now you may walk back to the time you began to hush, and receive choices in this present moment.

**Opening Portal: Ritual Invitation**

Breathe into your belly and connect to your body. Reclaim the voice that was never truly lost.
Consider one or more of the following ritual invitations to ground and open:

• Echo Chamber — In a private space, say out loud what you weren't allowed to say. Feel the vibration in your chest.

• Word Flow — Free-write for 3 minutes on the sentence: "What I never said was…"

• Throat Balm — Sip warm water with lemon or honey. Let your throat soften with each sip. Hum afterward.

These rituals may support you whenever your voice feels distant or buried.

## Scene One: The Silencing

You used to speak without filter.
As a child. As a dreamer. As a truth-teller.

But somewhere along the way…

you learned to pause.
To weigh your words.
To read the room first.

You made yourself digestible.
Palatable. Quiet.

And maybe it kept the peace.
But it cost your clarity.
Your authenticity.
Your voice.

And your body?
It remembers.

Tightness in the throat.
A flutter in the chest.
A pressure behind the eyes.

It's not just that you stopped speaking.
It's that you forgot what you wanted to say.

Until now.

**A Sacred Invitation to Choose Your Path**

Stay Silent — Keep your truth tucked away. → Go to Scene
Two A on page 27

Speak Softly — Share, but with caution. → Go to Scene Two
B on page 28

Speak Fully — Let it all out. → Go to Scene Two C on page 29

---

## Scene Two A: The Quiet One

You hold your words behind your teeth.

You nod when you disagree.

You smile instead of speak.

It is safer this way — but it is also lonelier.

The silence thickens inside your chest, like smoke with no exit.

Your body becomes the container for all the unsaid things.

Your throat tightens. Your jaw aches. Your heart whispers: I am still here.

You wonder: is silence protection… or prison?

If you stay within the experience of self-censorship, go to Path A at the end of this chapter, or…

If silence feels safer than truth, turn to Chapter 11: The Chamber of Contracts on page 75,

Or perhaps…

You find a locked box in your throat. If you open it, leap to Chapter 13: The Chamber of Treasures on page 89.

---

## Scene Two B: The Careful Speaker

You speak, but with filters.

You soften the edges.

You edit as you go.

You walk on eggshells, never sure which word may trigger an explosion.

Each sentence is measured. Polished. Small.

Your voice exists, but only in fragments — a puzzle missing pieces.

And yet… something inside sparks. Because even a half-truth is still a crack in the dam.

One day, you may let the whole river flow.

If you stay within the experience of partial expression, go to Path B at the end of this chapter, or…

If you're ready to practice honest expression, turn to Chapter 6: The Dance of Narcissus on page 37,

Or perhaps…

You find a microphone buried in the sand. If you pick it up, leap to Chapter 14: The Reclaiming on page 95.

---

## Scene Two C: The Unleashed Voice

You let it out.

The truth. The fear. The fury. The joy.

It comes out messy — but it's yours.

Your voice cracks, your face flushes, your body trembles...

And yet, it feels like the first full breath after years of holding your lungs too tight.

The words no longer belong to anyone else's script.

They are raw. They are wild. They are alive.

And you — you are alive with them.

If you stay within the experience of full expression, go to Path C at the end of this chapter, or...

If you're ready to anchor your voice in truth, turn to Chapter 9: The Reckoning of Projection on page 61,

Or perhaps...

You shout into the wind. A condor answers. If you follow it, leap to Chapter 10: The Chamber of Wounds on page 67.

# Chapter 4: Paths A, B, & C

**Path A** — You held it in. Again. The truth stayed trapped behind your teeth. And while safety wrapped itself around you, so did loneliness. Your body remembers what it wanted to say. Your throat aches. The silence grows louder. This is not failure. This is survival.

From here, you may continue directly forward into Chapter 5: The Disappearing Act

**Path B** — You spoke — even if softly. Even if only to test the waters. The body sighs with relief. The heart whispers: *Thank you for trying.* The new choice may be to let your "no" land with clarity or to let your laughter spill out, uncontained.

You are remembering that your voice is medicine.

From here, you may continue directly forward into Chapter 5: The Disappearing Act

**Path C** — You let it out — all of it. The voice that was once buried now rises like wildfire. Messy. Beautiful. Alive. And you realize: your words were never just yours. They were meant to ripple outward, to awaken, to remind.

You are not finding your voice. You are remembering it.

From here, you may continue directly forward into Chapter 5: The Disappearing Act

# Chapter 5: The Disappearing Act

You arrive at The Disappearing Act, where the slow erasure of self comes into focus — not through tragedy, but through habit, silence, and the subtle art of making oneself small. This chapter honors the quiet heartbreak of vanishing to keep the peace… and the sacred courage it takes to reappear.

**Opening Portal: Ritual Invitation**

Breathe into your belly and connect to your body. Let yourself come into view.
Consider one or more of the following ritual invitations to ground and open:

• Mirror Presence — Look into your own eyes for 60 seconds. Whisper: "I see you."

• Weight Offering — Place a stone in each hand. Feel the burden of roles you carry. Set them down, one by one.

• Name Recall — Write down all the roles you've performed in life (e.g. peacemaker, performer, ghost). Circle one that no longer serves you.

These rituals may become allies as you reappear — again and again — on the path ahead.

## Scene One: The Vanishing

You don't even notice it at first.
The way you shrink a little in each room.
The way you defer, stay agreeable, choose quiet.

You call it "not a big deal."
You call it "being easy."
You call it "avoiding conflict."

But the truth is… you've been ghosting yourself.

Your preferences fade.
Your desires go silent.
You start asking *What do they want from me?* instead of *What do I need right now?*

And your body?
It whispers the truth.

Your shoulders round inward.
Your voice softens to a whisper.
Your breath becomes careful.

You shape-shift.
You stay small.
You disappear — not dramatically, but gradually.

Until one day, someone says,
"I just love how low-maintenance you are."
And something inside you flinches.

Because deep down…
you don't want to be "easy"
If it means you cannot be real.

You want to reappear in true authenticity.

**A Sacred Invitation to Choose Your Path**

Stay Small — Remain agreeable. Invisible. "Good." → Go to Scene Two A below

Search for Yourself — Get curious about what's been buried. → Go to Scene Two B on page 34

Avoid It Entirely — Shut down and float away. → Go to Scene Two C on page 35

---

## Scene Two A: The Small Self

You agree again. You make yourself accommodating again.

And it works. People like you. The peace is kept. The waters stay calm.

But when the room empties, you feel hollow. Approval sits in your lap, but love is nowhere to be found.

If you stay within the experience of disappearing, go to Path A at the end of this chapter, or...

If you've confused love with approval, turn to Chapter 8: The Shame Spiral on page 53,

Or perhaps...

A child in a dream says, "Where did you go?". If you feel your heart wants to answer, leap to Chapter 11: The Chamber of Contracts on page 75.

---

## Scene Two B: The Turning Inward

This time, you pause. Your hand trembles as it lands on your chest. You whisper, *What do I want?*

At first, your mind is blank. But your breath deepens. Your ribs expand, stretching space where there was none. And beneath the stillness — a flicker. A faint yes.

Your eyes sting as tears rise uninvited. Your throat loosens, as though a door has cracked open. Your spine straightens.

It doesn't look dramatic from the outside. But from the inside? It's revolutionary. You remember: being seen begins with seeing yourself.

If you stay within the experience of reclaiming presence, go to Path B at the end of this chapter, or...

If you're ready to feel worthy of being seen, turn to Chapter 14: The Reclaiming on page 95,

Or perhaps...

You remember a nickname you had as a child. If you reminisce about it, leap to Chapter 13: The Chamber of Treasures on page 89.

---

## Scene Two C: The Float Away

You nod politely. You laugh at the right times. But inside, you are gone. Your eyes glaze over. Your breath grows shallow.

From the outside, you look fine. But from the inside, you've evaporated. Each time you float away, your body grows colder, your chest hollower. You wonder if anyone notices that you've left the room without moving a muscle.

If you stay within the experience of floating away, go to Path C at the end of this chapter, or…

If you fear visibility, but long for it too, turn to Chapter 6: The Dance of Narcissus on page 37,

Or perhaps…

You find an old photo where you're beaming with joy. You barely recognize yourself. If you want to reminisce, leap to Chapter 12: The Chamber of Grace on page 81.

# Chapter 5: Paths A, B, & C

---

**Path A** — You stayed small. And that's okay. Re-emergence cannot be rushed. Safety was the choice today.

From here, you may continue directly forward into Chapter 6: The Dance of Narcissus

---

**Path B** — You chose to re-enter. You remembered that you are not a role — you are a being. This is the start of presence.

From here, you may continue directly forward into Chapter 6: The Dance of Narcissus

---

**Path C** — You disappeared — but even absence holds a thread of return. Even in the dark, a light remains.

From here, you may continue directly forward into Chapter 6: The Dance of Narcissus

# Chapter 6: The Dance of Narcissus

This is the world of mirrors. Projection, reflection, self-image — all ripple across the surface of perception. We meet ourselves in the gaze of others, sometimes distorted, sometimes luminous. The Dance of Narcissus is not vanity — it is the longing to be seen, the ache of recognition, and the invitation to discover what is true beneath the reflection.

### Opening Portal: Ritual Invitation

Breathe into your belly and soften the need to be perceived a certain way.
Consider one or more of the following ritual invitations to ground and open:

• Bare Gaze — Look into a mirror and ask, "Who am I when no one is watching?"

• Shadow Scroll — Browse your own photos. Notice when you were performing… and when you were true.

• Water Drop Truth — Whisper a truth into a bowl of water. Watch it ripple. Let the mirror of water reflect what you're ready to receive.

These rituals may return to steady you each time you meet the mirror — within yourself or another.

## Scene One: The First Reflection

You are face-to-face with a mirror.

Not glass — but life itself.

A comment lands.

Maybe careless, maybe cruel.

It pierces. Your body contracts.

In a heartbeat, your mind scrambles:

They don't see me. They've misunderstood. I have to set it straight. Or maybe… it's their fault. Or maybe… I should just swallow it and disappear.

The mirror gleams with possibility.

It does not flatter, nor condemn — it simply reflects. And in its reflection, your nervous system begins its old choreography: fight, fling, flee.

But this time, you pause.

It is about what you cannot yet see…
in yourself.

The mirror waits.

How will you meet it?

**A Sacred Invitation to Choose Your Path**

Defend — Raise your armor. Argue, justify, prove your worth. → Go to Scene Two A on page 39

Project — Cast the sting outward. Blame, distort, accuse. → Go to Scene Two B on page 40

Shift — Catch yourself mid-pattern and turn toward something new. → Go to Scene Two C on page 41

## Scene Two A: The Defender

The words leap from your lips before you can stop them.

Quick. Sharp. Righteous.

You stand taller, chest tight, determined to rewrite the image they hold of you.

And for a moment, it works — the mirror seems to bend beneath your will.

But then the echo returns: hollow, restless.

Who are you trying to convince? Them... or yourself?

The mirror fractures.

One shard shows the strong one. Another, the clever one. Another, the perfect one.

Yet behind them all shivers the unarmored self — tender, trembling, asking: Will you ever lay down the sword and let me be seen?

If you stay behind this wall, go to Path A at the end of this chapter, or...

If defensiveness often rises in you, turn to Chapter 10 — The Chamber of Wounds on page 67,

Or perhaps...

The mirror ripples and becomes water. If you swim into it, leap to Chapter 3 — The Allure of Escape on page 19.

---

## Scene Two B: The Projector

The sting is unbearable, so you hurl it outward.

"You never listen."

"You're the one who twists everything."

"You made me this way."

The fire feels good at first — hot, alive, powerful.

But it burns through quickly.

And when the smoke clears, the mirror is still there… and the face staring back is still yours.

Projection buys you time, but it does not buy you freedom. The reflection always circles back home.

If you are ready to feel to heal, go to Path B at the end of this chapter, or…

To explore distortion turn to Chapter 9 — The Reckoning of Projection on page 61,

Or perhaps…

The reflection softens into the face of your inner child. If you follow, leap to Chapter 7 — The Mirror Break on page 45.

---

## Scene Two C: The Shift

The triggered reflex rises — defend, project, disappear. You know this dance.

But instead of reacting, you pause.

You take one long, slow breath…the sacred pause.

A flicker of recognition comes: Ah. Here it is again. The mirror. The old pattern.

And with that recognition, space opens.

You smile, not the mask-smile, but a quiet one that says: I see you. And I choose something else.

The mirror softens. Its edges blur. It becomes less cage, more teacher.

You are not reacting. You are choosing a compassionate response. And that changes everything.

If you go deeper into the awakening of your essence, go to Path C at the end of this chapter, or…

If curiosity of the sacred pause stirs, follow this conscious noticing into Chapter 12 — The Chamber of Grace on page 81,

Or perhaps…

The mirror reveals a serpent coiled at your feet. If you follow its path, leap to Chapter 11 — The Chamber of Contracts on page 75.

# Chapter 6: Paths A, B, & C

**Path A** — You defended again. You sought to be right, to be seen through another's eyes. And that's okay. The mirror will return. It always does. This is not failure. This is meant. You may begin again.

From here, you may continue directly forward into Chapter 7: The Mirror Break

**Path B** — You cast the sting outward. For a moment, it gave you strength. But strength without self-reflection grows brittle. The mirror waits patiently for your gaze to return.

From here, you may continue directly forward into Chapter 7: The Mirror Break

**Path C** — You noticed the dance. You stepped aside instead of looping in circles. This small turn is enormous — every noticing loosens the grip of the old pattern. You are not the reflection. You are the one who sees.

From here, you may continue directly forward into Chapter 7: The Mirror Break

# Chapter 7: The Mirror Break

The mirror does not lie, but neither does it show the whole. What you see reflected is only a shard of truth — fractured by the stories you've been told and the ones you've told yourself. The breaking of the mirror is not your ruin. It is your release.

### Opening Portal: Ritual Invitation

Breathe into your belly and connect to your body. You are the courage to see clearly.
Consider one or more of the following ritual invitations to ground and open:

• Fragment Finder — Take a blank page. Write: "The stories I've told about who I am…" and list them. Circle what no longer fits.

• Broken Mirror Meditation — Visualize a cracked mirror. Breathe slowly as the pieces begin to fall away. What remains?

• Light Reveal — Sit in dim light with a candle. Ask: What truth am I ready to see that I've been avoiding?

These rituals can return anytime the reflection feels distorted… or when clarity longs to rise.

## Scene One: The Fracture

The moment arrives quietly.
One small crack — a word, a gesture, a look that pierces deeper than expected.

At first, it seems harmless. Just a fissure across the smooth glass. But the crack spreads. It multiplies. The mirror that once held you together can no longer contain the weight.

Shards scatter across the floor of your mind. You see yourself reflected in fragments — one piece smiling, another scowling, another turned away in shame. Each piece tells a different story of who you are.

You kneel to gather them, desperate to restore the image, but the glass cuts your palms. Your efforts draw blood. The harder you try to hold it all, the more it hurts.

This was the mirror you trusted. The one that told you who to be. The one that showed you the mask, polished and acceptable.

Now it lies in pieces.

And here, in the silence after the shatter, a question rises: If the mirror no longer defines you… who are you?

The air feels heavy, yet strangely open. For the first time, there is space beyond the reflection.

Perhaps the breaking was never a failure — but an invitation.

**A Sacred Invitation to Choose Your Path**

Glue the Mirror — Pretend nothing changed. → Go to Scene Two A on page 47

Look Closer — Study what's emerging. → Go to Scene Two B on page 48

Walk Through — Let the old reflection fall away. → Go to Scene Two C on page 49

---

## Scene Two A: The Repair

You reach for the glue.

For the old story.

For the certainty of what you've always believed.

The pieces almost fit.

If you press hard enough, the cracks blur.

If you squint, it looks whole again.

But something is missing.

The mirror might hold — but only by hiding the light.

The reflection becomes safer, smaller, duller.

You wonder: is survival worth dimming what wants to shine?

If you stay within the experience of repair and denial, go to Path A at the end of this chapter, or…

If familiar stories still run the show, turn to Chapter 2: The Masked Beginning on page 13,

Or perhaps…

A beam of light slips through the crack and forms a doorway. If you step through, leap to Chapter 14: The Reclaiming on page 95

---

## Scene Two B: The Seer

You lean in.

Not to fix — but to witness.

The mirror no longer frightens you.

It reveals what's been waiting: grief long silenced, relief like an exhale, and a truer outline of your life.

It's jagged.

It's unfinished.

But it's real.

Your eyes water — not from pain alone, but from recognition.

Here is the story beneath the story.

Here is the you that was hidden in plain sight.

It's not perfect — but it's honest.

If you stay within the experience of sober clarity, go to Path B at the end of this chapter, or...

If clarity reveals an old pact, turn to Chapter 11: The Chamber of Contracts on page 75,

Or perhaps...

A feather lands on the glass and points south. If you step in this direction of the serpent, leap to Chapter 10: The Chamber of Wounds on page 67.

---

## Scene Two C: The Passage

You stop fixing.

You stop analyzing.

You begin walking.

Through the broken image.

Through the fracture.

Into the room behind it.

At first, it feels like trespassing —

but then, like returning.

The floor is raw stone.

The air is heavy with silence.

And yet... every step feels truer than any reflection ever did.

You realize: you are not walking toward truth.

You are walking with it.

It's raw — and you're ready.

If you stay within the experience of courageous transition, go to Path C at the end of this chapter, or...

If truth wants embodiment, go to Chapter 12: The Chamber of Grace on page 81,

Or perhaps...

A butterfly glides alongside you. If you smile at it, leap to Chapter 13: The Chamber of Treasures on page 89.

# Chapter 7: Paths A, B, & C

**Path A** — You patched the old story. It may hold a little longer, but light keeps finding you.

From here, you may continue directly forward into Chapter 8: The Shame Spiral

**Path B** — You looked with steady eyes. Honesty softened you into a deeper compassion.

From here, you may continue directly forward into Chapter 8: The Shame Spiral

**Path C** — You crossed the threshold. A new landscape of Self is now opening.

From here, you may continue directly forward into Chapter 8: The Shame Spiral

# Chapter 8: The Shame Spiral

Shame is a spiral staircase leading nowhere. It coils tight around the body until you forget there was ever a door out. Yet even in shame's grip, a quiet knowing remains: you are not the spiral. You are the sky it curls within.

**Opening Portal: Ritual Invitation**

Breathe into your belly and connect to radical gentleness in your whole body.
Consider one or more of the following ritual invitations to ground and open:

• Hand on Heart — Breathe and whisper: "Even this part belongs."

• Truth Receipt — Write three things you're ashamed of. Then add a second line: "And I am still worthy."

• Soft Exhale — Inhale for 4, exhale for 6. Let the body speak safety back to the mind.

Perhaps return to these rituals whenever shame starts to spiral.

## Scene One: The Tightening

It begins with a flush of heat. A voice inside whispers: Wrong. Your chest caves, your stomach knots, your throat closes.

You try to swallow it down, but shame is clever. It crawls into the corners of your body, hides behind your ribs, coils around your hips. Every breath becomes shallow. Every thought sharpens into accusation.

I shouldn't have said that.
I shouldn't have wanted that.
I am too much.
I am not enough.

Shame is not only a feeling — it is a forgetting. A forgetting of your belonging. A forgetting of your wholeness.

It doesn't even need others to enforce it anymore. The voices that once silenced you live on in your own mind. They've been rehearsed so long, they sound like truth.

You look down. You hide. You shrink.
The spiral tightens.

And yet — in the deepest coil, there is a pause. A heartbeat. A shimmer.

Something in you remembers: this spiral was a learned limiting belief. Which means it can be shifted.

The question becomes: will you keep spinning, or will you dare to lift your gaze?

**A Sacred Invitation to Choose Your Path**

Hide the Part — Disappear until it passes. → Go to Scene Two A on page 55

Stay with Kindness — Sit beside the shame and listen. → Go to Scene Two B on page 56

Offer it to Grace — Let love hold what judgment cannot. →
Go to Scene Two C on page 57

---

## Scene Two A: The Cloak

You tuck your authenticity away.

You work harder, smile bigger, act fine.

On the outside, you sparkle.

On the inside, you vanish.

The world applauds the mask, but your chest knows the truth — the ache doesn't disappear, it only burrows deeper.

Shame quiets for a moment — but only because you left yourself again.

The hiding feels safe, even familiar.

But with every concealment, your light grows harder to find.

If you stay within the experience of concealment, go to Path A at the end of this chapter, or…

If hiding has become home, turn to Chapter 5: The Disappearing Act on page 31,

Or perhaps…

You find a cloak that makes you invisible. If you remove it, leap to Chapter 14: The Reclaiming on page 95.

---

## Scene Two B: The Companion

You sit beside the ache like you would a child.

You don't fix.

You don't flee.

You stay.

The air grows softer around you.

Your body eases into presence.

The ache trembles — then settles, as if surprised to be met without demand.

You begin to see: the spiral doesn't dissolve when controlled.

It loosens when witnessed.

When you bring the warmth of your own company, loneliness becomes less lonely.

If you stay within the experience of compassionate presence, go to Path B at the end of this chapter, or...

If tenderness is awakening, turn to Chapter 12: The Chamber of Grace on page 81,

Or perhaps…

A small flame refuses to go out. If you cup it with your hands, leap to Chapter 13: The Chamber of Treasures on page 89.

---

## Scene Two C: The Rain

You offer the shame to something larger.

Prayer. Breath. Earth.

You let it leave your body and enter the vastness.

And in that surrender, something shifts.

Not fixed — but freed.

As if the weight was never meant to be carried alone.

You feel the invisible arms of what holds all things — life itself, the Great Mother, the unseen web that whispers: you belong even here.

The rain falls. The ground softens.

You remember that even shame, when given back, becomes fertile.

If you stay within the experience of being received, go to Path C at the end of this chapter, or…

If devotion soothes your nervous system, turn to Chapter 10: The Chamber of Wounds on page 67,

Or perhaps...

Rain begins and the world smells new. If you dance in the rain, leap to Chapter 11: The Chamber of Contracts on page 75.

# Chapter 8: Paths A, B, & C

**Path A** — You hid again. The spiral quieted — but so did you. Presence will call you back when you're ready.

From here, you may continue directly forward into Chapter 9: The Reckoning of Projection

**Path B** — You stayed with tenderness. Shame softened into something human and divine.

From here, you may continue directly forward into Chapter 9: The Reckoning of Projection

**Path C** — You offered it to love. Grace held what judgment could not.

From here, you may continue directly forward into Chapter 9: The Reckoning of Projection

# Chapter 9: The Reckoning of Projection

You now enter The Reckoning of Projection — the moment the mirror sharpens. Walk within to reveal the subtle and sacred ways fears, longing, and wounds are projected onto others. It invites a shift from blame to ownership, from illusion to insight, and to meet oneself in the reflections previously judged.

**Opening Portal: Ritual Invitation**

Breathe into your belly and connect to your body. Let reflection soften, not shame you.
Consider one or more of the following ritual invitations:

• Mirror Write — Think of someone who triggers you. Write: "What if this is a mirror for…" and complete the sentence.

• Projection Burn — Write what you've blamed others for, then burn the paper with intention: *I reclaim this part of me.*

• Ripple Meditation — Imagine your emotions as ripples in water. Watch how they reach others… and return.

These rituals may return anytime the outer world feels louder than your inner truth.

## Scene One: The Mirror Revealed

It's so easy to see what they're doing wrong.
So clear.
So obvious.

You feel it in your body — the anger, the judgment, the frustration.
*Why are they like that?*
*Why don't they change?*

And then it happens.
A pause.
A glimpse.
A whisper:
*Is this about them… or is this about me?*

You flinch.
You breathe.
You trace the thread.

And it brings you not to blame, but to insight.

You've been casting shadows.
You've been scattering yourself onto the screen of others.
Longing to be loved.
Terrified to be seen.
Desperate to avoid what hurts.

But the mirror doesn't lie.
It reflects.
And now… you're ready to look.

**A Sacred Invitation to Choose Your Path**

Stay in Blame — It's safer to focus on them. → Go to Scene Two A below

Get Curious — What if this is about you, too? → Go to Scene Two B on page 64

Avoid It All — Scroll, vent, distract. → Go to Scene Two C on page 65

---

# Scene Two A: The Externalizer

You vent to a friend.
You make your case.
You catalog their flaws.

And for a moment... it helps.

But deep down, you know:
The freedom you seek doesn't live in their behavior.
It lives in your awareness.

If you stay within the experience of blame, go to Path A at the end of this chapter, or...

If you're ready to own what you see in others, turn to Chapter 10: The Chamber of Wounds on page 67,

Or perhaps…

You dream of shouting at a stranger, only to find it's your own voice yelling back. If you respond, leap to Chapter 13: The Chamber of Treasures on page 89.

---

## Scene Two B: The Liberation

You pause.
You breathe.
You ask: What does this reflect in me?

And it stings, because it rings — but it also liberates.

You reclaim a lost piece.
You stop outsourcing your pain.
You begin to walk yourself home.

If you stay within the experience of integration, go to Path B at the end of this chapter, or…

If you're ready to rewrite the contract behind the wound, turn to Chapter 11: The Chamber of Contracts on page 75,

Or perhaps…

A condor lands on a branch and looks you in the eye. You see a celebration. If you deepen the eye gaze, leap to Chapter 12: The Chamber of Grace on page 81

---

## Scene Two C: The Distractor

You clean the kitchen.
You binge a show.
You disappear into busyness.

It's easier than seeing.
Safer than feeling.

But the trigger remains…
Waiting to be loved into light.

If you stay within the experience of avoidance, go to Path C at the end of this chapter, or…

If distraction has dulled your truth, turn to Chapter 3: The Allure of Escape on page 19,

Or perhaps…

You see yourself in every passerby, until you no longer feel separate. If you explore this oneness, leap to Chapter 14: The Reclaiming on page 95.

# Chapter 9: Paths A, B, & C

**Path A** — You chose blame. And that's okay. Projection is a teacher — and it will wait for you to look again.

From here, you may continue directly forward into Chapter 10: The Chamber of Wounds

**Path B** — You reclaimed your reflection. You saw yourself — and chose compassion.

From here, you may continue directly forward into Chapter 10: The Chamber of Wounds

**Path C** — You turned away — but truth has a pulse. And it will rise again.

From here, you may continue directly forward into Chapter 10: The Chamber of Wounds

# Chapter 10: The Chamber of Wounds

You arrive at The Chamber of Wounds — the sacred hollow where the deepest pain is neither avoided nor explained, but held. This chapter does not ask you to relive the wound, but to re-meet it — with the compassion that was missing the first time.

**Opening Portal: Ritual Invitation**

Breathe into your belly and connect to your body. The wound is ready to be seen by someone safe — you.

Consider one or more of the following ritual invitations:

• Witness Letter — Write a letter to your younger self who endured the wound. Say what they needed to hear.

• Body Listening — Sit in silence and ask your body: "Where does the wound live?" Place your hand there. Just breathe.

• Mirror Hug — Sit before a mirror. Look into your own eyes and imagine the child you once were. Wrap your arms around yourself and whisper: "I'm here now. I won't leave you."

These rituals may return whenever your pain resurfaces or longs to be honored.

## Scene One: The Looping

You didn't think you'd have to come back here.

You've done "the work".

You've healed so much.

You've moved on.

But an ache remains.

Not always loud. But steady.

And part of you knows — it's time.

Remember what happened. Trust and surrender. Let it come forward to be witnessed and honored.

And then…

The memory returns. Not with violence, but invitation.

Softness. Safety. Tenderness.

The room. The moment. The look. The words. The absence.

It's the same loop you've walked before.

The echo of pain that circles back, asking the same question:

Will anyone come for me this time?

You descend into the hollow of what hurt.

And this time… you don't abandon yourself.

You stay.

You breathe.

You remember: the wound is not a trap, but a threshold.

And the soul? It stirs.

Because you are not broken. You never were.

You are birthing a deeper wholeness.

A wholeness that comes when the child is finally met.

## A Sacred Invitation to Choose Your Path

Close the Door — Not now. Not ready. → Go to Scene Two A below

Enter Gently — Sit beside the wound. Listen. → Go to Scene Two B on page 70

Honor the Child — Reparent the younger you. → Go to Scene Two C on page 71

---

# Scene Two A: The Avoidance

You retreat.

You distract.

You tell yourself: another time.

And that's okay.
The wound will wait. Love is patient.

If you stay within the experience of avoidance, go to Path A at the end of this chapter, or...

If the ache resurfaces in silence, turn to Chapter 5: The Disappearing Act on page 31,

Or perhaps...

You dream of a locked door in your childhood home. A voice says: "You are the key." If you turn the doorknob, leap to Chapter 14: The Reclaiming on page 95.

---

## Scene Two B: The Witnessing

You stay.

You breathe.

You place your hand on your chest.

And whisper: "I see you. I believe you. I'm not leaving."

The wound softens — not because it's gone, but because it is no longer alone.

If you stay within the experience of witnessing, go to Path B at the end of this chapter, or...

If the pain softened your heart, turn to Chapter 12: The Chamber of Grace on page 81,

Or perhaps...

You meet an old version of yourself. They place a crystal in your hand. If you accept it, leap to Chapter 13: The Chamber of Treasures on page 89.

---

## Scene Two C: The Reparenting

You see them.

The small one — wide eyes, trembling, waiting.

No one came then.

But you are here now.

You kneel.

You open your arms.

You say: "I've got you. I always will."

The child melts into your chest.

The wound becomes a bridge.

And the love that was missing is restored through you.

For a moment, safety returns.

A deep, calming breath the child never got to take — they take now, through you.

And yet… the wound also whispers.

This is not the end. The old promises, the old contracts, still live in me.

You know: this is the beginning.

The cycle of abandonment has cracked, and now comes the chance to rewrite the story.

If you stay within the experience of reparenting, go to Path C at the end of this chapter, or…

If the embrace stirs a longing for deeper union, turn to Chapter 12: The Chamber of Grace on page 81,

Or perhaps…

The child places a drawing in your hand — a sun with rays reaching everywhere. If you follow its light, leap to Chapter 15: The New Myth on page 103.

# Chapter 10: Paths A, B, & C

**Path A** — You weren't ready. And that's sacred, too. The wound will call again — when safety returns.

From here, you may continue directly forward into Chapter 11: The Chamber of Contracts

**Path B** — You stayed. You listened. And the healing began — not by force, but by love.

From here, you may continue directly forward into Chapter 11: The Chamber of Contracts

**Path C** — You reparented with compassion. Not fully, not completely — but you began. You offered presence to the child within, and the cycle of abandonment cracked open. This is the first step in becoming the guardian you always needed.

From here, you may continue directly forward into Chapter 11: The Chamber of Contracts

# Chapter 11: The Chamber of Contracts

You now enter The Chamber of Contracts — the sacred space where the soul's silent vows live. This chapter invites you to examine the promises you made in moments of pain or protection — and to ask whether it's time to keep them, rewrite them, or alchemize them.

### Opening Portal: Ritual Invitation

Breathe into your belly and sense these contracts were made with love. They may be let go with love.
Consider one or more of the following ritual invitations:

• Contract Reading — Write: "I once promised myself…" and see what surfaces. Speak it aloud. Decide if it still serves.

• Cord Cut — Visualize an energetic thread tied to an old vow. With breath or movement, symbolically sever it.

• Salt Soak — Bathe your hands or feet in salt water. As the tension softens, say: "I am free to choose again."

These rituals may return when old patterns pull you toward old pacts.

## Scene One: The Signature

You didn't realize you signed it. There was no pen, no paper.

Just a moment.

A wound.

A fear.

And then a vow:

*Never again.*
*Always.*
*I have to…*

Maybe it was after betrayal.

Maybe after being silenced.

Maybe it came from needing to survive.

You became loyal to that contract.

And it shaped your choices.

It shaped your relationships.

It shaped your sense of self.

What was the original wound?

What was written on that contract as protection?

And now you feel the tension.

The contract no longer fits.

And the soul is stirring…

Is it ready to rewrite? To burn? To dissolve?

### A Sacred Invitation to Choose Your Path

Obey the Contract — Stay loyal. Stay safe. Stay where you are. → Go to Scene Two A below

Re-negotiate — Speak with the part of you who made it. → Go to Scene Two B on page 78

Avoid — Pretend the contract doesn't exist. → Go to Scene Two C on page 79

---

## Scene Two A: The Enforcer

You follow the rules.

You keep the contract.

And life stays familiar.

But something inside aches — the cost of this agreement is your freedom.

If you stay within the experience of self-limitation, go to Path A at the end of this chapter, or...

If you're ready to dissolve what no longer serves, turn to Chapter 10: The Chamber of Wounds on page 67,

Or perhaps...

In a dream, you see your name written in fire. If you watch it alchemize into smoke, leap to Chapter 13: The Chamber of Treasures on page 89.

---

## Scene Two B: The Re-negotiation

You meet the version of yourself who made the vow.

You listen without judgment.

You thank them.

And together, you release the pact.

A new promise emerges — not from fear, but from truth.

If you stay within the experience of conscious rewriting, go to Path B at the end of this chapter, or...

If you're ready to honor the original wound, turn to Chapter 10: The Chamber of Wounds on page 67,

Or perhaps...

You unroll a scroll written in stars. It fades as you breathe. If you are ready to feel peace with this, leap to Chapter 12: The Chamber of Grace on page 81.

## Scene Two C: The Denial

You sense the contract... but turn away.

You pretend not to know.

You tell yourself: this is just how I am.

I have to be this way. I don't need to change. I shouldn't have to.

And yet... you still feel bound.

If you stay within the experience of resistance, go to Path C at the end of this chapter, or...

If your avoidance feels too familiar, turn to Chapter 5: The Disappearing Act on page 31,

Or perhaps...

You see a bird circling above a locked gate. You notice a key is in your hand. If you try the key in the lock, leap to Chapter 14: The Reclaiming on page 95.

# Chapter 11: Paths A, B, & C

---

**Path A** — You honored the contract. For now, it still feels safer. But a new truth is beginning to form.

From here, you may continue directly forward into Chapter 12: The Chamber of Grace

---

**Path B** — You rewrote the vow. You chose again — with consciousness. The soul begins to move with more freedom. What does the new contract say?

From here, you may continue directly forward into Chapter 12: The Chamber of Grace

---

**Path C** — You denied the contract. But even buried agreements can shape the road ahead if nothing new is forged. It will call again.

From here, you may continue directly forward into Chapter 12: The Chamber of Grace

# Chapter 12: The Chamber of Grace

You now enter The Chamber of Grace — the quiet sanctuary beyond effort. Here, healing is not earned but received. The parts of you once hidden or forgotten begin to return…soul fragments stir and find their way home, weaving themselves back into the fabric of your being…welcomed by gentleness rather than striving. Let love meet you exactly where you are… arising from within and filling you completely.

### Opening Portal: Ritual Invitation

Breathe grace into your whole body. Let it arrive.
Consider one or more of the following ritual invitations:

• Stillness Sit — Light a candle. Sit without fixing or thinking. Just let yourself be.

• Grace Letter — Write a letter from Grace to you. Let the words be gentle. Let them surprise you.

• Soul Piece Drawing — Draw (or write) a symbol for a part of you that's returning. Ask what it needs to stay.

These rituals may return whenever effort has replaced embodiment.

## Scene One: The Softening

You feel tired.

Not just from doing — but from becoming.

Always reaching.

Always growing.

Always healing.

And now?

Now you just want to rest.

And rest, it turns out, is delicious.

Like sunlight curling on your skin.

Like the first sip of cool water after a long walk.

Like laughter that bubbles up for no reason at all.

For so long, stillness felt dangerous.

If you stopped, would everything fall apart?

But in the pause… nothing breaks.

In fact, the world keeps holding you.

The air feels softer, as if it has been waiting.

The earth sighs beneath you, welcoming your weight.

Even your shoulders join the party, finally dropping.

You're not being graded here.

You're not on trial.

You're simply… here.

This is not the chapter of effort.

It is the chapter of grace.

And grace?

She's both playful and loving.

She slips in without knocking.

She twirls you around the kitchen when you least expect it.

She shows up with flowers you didn't plant and songs you don't remember learning.

You remember: worth was never in question.

You remember: presence is enough.

You remember: joy is medicine, too.

The river giggles over stones without asking you to push.

The flower opens because it feels good.

The sky holds itself just fine without your effort.

And your heart?

It doesn't need to prove a thing.

The softening is not surrendering the dance.

It is remembering that you are the music.

A lost part of you has returned.

### A Sacred Invitation to Choose Your Path

Resist the Rest — Try to stay busy. Prove your worth. → Go to Scene Two A below

Receive the Grace — Let it in. Let it soften you. → Go to Scene Two B on page 85

Perform Healing — Pretend you're past this. Smile through it. → Go to Scene Two C on page 86

---

## Scene Two A: The Resistor

You try to do more.
Fix more.
Prove more.

But it leaves you emptier.

Grace doesn't follow force.

It follows surrender.

If you stay within the experience of striving, go to Path A at the end of this chapter, or…

If worth still feels tied to doing, turn to Chapter 2: The Masked Beginning on page 13,

Or perhaps…

You dream of floating in water. A voice says: "Nothing is required." If you deepen into the dream, leap to Chapter 14: The Reclaiming on page 95.

---

## Scene Two B: The Receiving

You rest.
You weep.
You laugh.
You breathe.

And you feel it:

A presence that holds you.

A grace that asks nothing.

A return to being.

If you stay within the experience of grace, go to Path B at the end of this chapter, or...

If wholeness has begun to rise, turn to Chapter 13: The Chamber of Treasures on page 89,

Or perhaps...

Two hummingbirds settle in a tree nearby. If you're ready to explore the energy of the cosmos, leap to Chapter 15: The New Myth on page 103.

## Scene Two C: The Performer

You smile through the pain.

You say the right things.

You spiritualize the ache.

But grace doesn't need performance.

It needs presence.

If you stay within the experience of bypass, go to Path C at the end of this chapter, or...

If you're ready to stop pretending, turn to Chapter 7: The Mirror Break on page 45,

Or perhaps...

A guacamayo lands on your shoulder. It sings the song you didn't know you missed. If you sing along, leap to Chapter 15: The New Myth on page 103.

# Chapter 12: Paths A, B, & C

**Path A** — You pushed through. But grace waits for the moment you stop. And she will find you then.

From here, you may continue directly forward into Chapter 13: The Chamber of Treasures

**Path B** — You let grace enter. And something softened — maybe for the first time in years. Be with this now...feel it in your heart...in your whole body.

From here, you may continue directly forward into Chapter 13: The Chamber of Treasures

**Path C** — You performed your healing. But healing doesn't need an audience. Only your presence.

From here, you may continue directly forward into Chapter 13: The Chamber of Treasures

# Chapter 13: The Chamber of Treasures

You now enter The Chamber of Treasures — the sacred return of what was never lost, only hidden. This chapter honors the soul parts that fractured in pain and now return bearing gifts. What you thought was broken... was medicine.

### Opening Portal: Ritual Invitation

Breathe into your belly...the medicine is already inside you. Consider one or more of the following ritual invitations:

• Power Object — Hold a stone, feather, or talisman. Breathe with it. Say: "I remember why you're here."

• Integration Breath — Inhale and visualize lost energy returning. Exhale and say: "I receive."

• Receive Something — A flower. A hug. A sip of tea. Let it be enough. Let it bless you.

These rituals may return whenever you feel scattered, unseen, or ready to reclaim.

## Scene One: The Return

There's something familiar in the air.
Not memory — essence.
Something once yours... coming back.

You feel it first in your chest.

A flutter.
A warmth.
A yes.

A lost treasure returns.
The voice once silenced.
The fierce boundary.
The innocent joy.

You thought you had to become someone else.
But healing… was always about *becoming more of who you
truly are*.

The treasure is not something new.
It's what you carried through the fire.

And now — it's time to remember.

**A Sacred Invitation to Choose Your Path**

Leave the Gifts — Not yet ready. Too much. → Go to Scene
Two A on page 91

Receive What's Yours — Welcome it back. Begin again. →
Go to Scene Two B on page 91

Distract with the Old Story — Avoid the new. Stay known.
→ Go to Scene Two C on page 92

## Scene Two A: The Reluctant One

You feel the return.
But it scares you.
What will change?
What will be asked?

You say: "Not yet."
And that is valid, too.

If you stay within the experience of hesitation, go to Path A
at the end of this chapter, or…

If change feels unsafe but true, turn to Chapter 6: The Dance
of Narcissus on page 37,

Or perhaps…

You see a treasure chest in the forest. A child beckons you to
open it. If you comply, leap to Chapter 15: The New Myth on
page 103.

## Scene Two B: The Reclaimer

You open your hands.
You say yes.
You received the part of you that once hid in the shadows.

And it brings power.
Wisdom.
A sacred tool. A gift. A symbol.

What does this treasure feel like? Look like? What is its purpose?

You are no longer fragmented.
You are no longer waiting.

If you stay within the experience of soul retrieval, go to Path B at the end of this chapter, or...

If you're ready to birth a new truth, turn to Chapter 15: The New Myth on page 103,

Or perhaps...

A serpent appears at your feet. If you feel called to follow the beauty way, leap to Chapter 16: The Trailhead on page 109.

---

## Scene Two C: The Story Loop

You go back to the old story.
You say: "That's just how I am."
You ignore the treasure... for now.

But it doesn't disappear.

It waits.

And it will return again — shining.

If you stay within the experience of resistance, go to Path C at the end of this chapter, or...

If old stories keep looping, turn to Chapter 9: The Reckoning of Projection on page 61,

Or perhaps...

You find a gold thread trailing from your pocket. It leads you to a forgotten doorway. If you open it, leap to Chapter 15: The New Myth on page 103.

# Chapter 13: Paths A, B, & C

---

**Path A** — You weren't ready to receive. And that's okay. The treasure waits — with patience and love.

From here, you may continue directly forward into Chapter 14: The Reclaiming

---

**Path B** — You received the gift. You welcomed the return. And now, something ancient within you has awakened.

From here, you may continue directly forward into Chapter 14: The Reclaiming

---

**Path C** — You returned to the familiar. But the gift remains — just beyond the next veil.

From here, you may continue directly forward into Chapter 14: The Reclaiming

# Chapter 14: The Reclaiming

You now evolve into The Reclaiming — the moment you return to yourself not as someone new, but as someone whole. This chapter invites you to step forward with clarity, integrity, and the power that was never truly lost.

### Opening Portal: Ritual Invitation

Breathe into your belly…you are not becoming — you are remembering.
Consider one or more of the following ritual invitations:

• Mirror Declaration — Look into your eyes. Speak the truth you've reclaimed. Say it three times.

• Embodiment Walk — Walk barefoot (if safe). Feel your presence return to your steps.

• Soul Statement — Write a single sentence that begins: "I now choose…" and carry it with you.

These rituals may return whenever you forget your power or voice.

## Scene One: The Emergence

It doesn't feel dramatic.

There is no spotlight.

No trumpet. No applause.

Just a breath.

A knowing.

A truth that lands deep and still.

You are here.

Not trying.

Not performing.

Not waiting for permission.

Just... here.

And in this presence, something shifts.

What was once exiled returns to the circle.

The silenced voice rises.

The forgotten body softens.

The fractured soul pieces rethread themselves into wholeness.

There is no rush.

No need to prove.

The power you thought you lost was only ever waiting to be welcomed back.

Your no becomes clear — not sharp, but steady.

Your yes becomes sacred — not desperate, but alive.

Your boundaries become holy ground — not walls, but thresholds.

And with each breath, you feel it more fully:

I don't have to earn my belonging.

I don't have to barter for my worth.

I never truly left myself —

I simply forgot the way back.

Now, you remember.

And the remembering feels like coming home.

**A Sacred Invitation to Choose Your Path**

Stay Hidden — Still too risky to be seen. → Go to Scene Two A below

Dance in Your Light — Walk forward in full presence. → Go to Scene Two B on page 98

Revert to Old Roles — It's safer to be who they expect. → Go to Scene Two C on page 99

---

# Scene Two A: The Hidden One

You've come so far.
But the world still feels unsafe.

So you tuck your power just beneath the surface.
You whisper when you want to roar.

And that's okay.
Visibility can be a trauma, too.

Hiding may protect the tender new growth of your becoming.
But it can also keep the garden from sunlight.

If you stay within the experience of cautious emergence, go to Path A at the end of this chapter, or...

If hiding has served its time, turn to Chapter 5: The Disappearing Act on page 31,

Or perhaps...

An eagle circles above. If you want to see what lies beyond the mountains, leap to Chapter 16: The Trailhead on page 109.

---

## Scene Two B: The Sovereign One

You speak clearly.
You stand fully.
You make no apology for your truth.

And not because it's perfect.
But because it's *yours*.

You share — and you do so with love.
Your light does not diminish others.
It invites them.

Sovereignty is not dominance.
It is alignment.
It is knowing that your energy, your very being is a gift.

If you stay within the experience of full reclamation, go to
Path B at the end of this chapter, or...

If sovereignty has awakened, turn to Chapter 15: The New
Myth on page 103,

Or perhaps...

A jaguar appears at your side. If you walk impeccably and
fearlessly with her, leap to Chapter 16: The Trailhead on page
109.

---

## Scene Two C: The Repeater

You try on the old roles.
The pleaser. The performer. The fixer.

They still fit — but they don't feel right.

At first, the familiarity comforts you.
But soon, you notice the tightness.

The false smile.

The ache.

You sense something stirring beneath them.
An invitation to stop pretending.

The roles once saved you.
Now they suffocate you.

If you stay within the experience of role relapse, go to Path C
at the end of this chapter, or...

If an identity feels outdated, turn to Chapter 2: The Masked
Beginning on page 13,

Or perhaps...

You find a costume hanging in your closet — you touch it. If
you're ready to shed this old layer, leap to Chapter 15: The
New Myth on page 103.

# Chapter 14: Paths A, B, & C

**Path A** — You stayed in the quiet. And that quiet is sacred. When you're ready to roar — the ground will hold you.

From here, you may continue directly forward into Chapter 15: The New Myth

**Path B** — You stood in your light. Fully. Boldly. Softly. And it was life-giving…the world turns more joyfully.

From here, you may continue directly forward into Chapter 15: The New Myth

**Path C** — You slipped into the old story. But something didn't fit. And now, you're ready to reclaim the pen.

From here, you may continue directly forward into Chapter 15: The New Myth

# Chapter 15: The New Myth

You now explore The New Myth — where the old stories dissolve and the sacred narrative of your becoming begins. This chapter invites you to choose, with love, power, and infinite possibility, the myth you now wish to live by.

### Opening Portal: Ritual Invitation

Breathe into your belly...the story is not fixed — it's forged. Consider one or more of the following ritual invitations:

• Rewrite — Take a piece of a painful story and rewrite its ending. Let your soul write, not your fear.

• Fire Speak — Speak aloud the old myths you're releasing. Burn them. Bury them. Free them.

• Choose Your Name — Whisper a new name, title, or role you are ready to explore.

These rituals may return whenever you forget that you are the author.

## Scene One: The Narrative Break

The old story no longer fits.
Not because it wasn't true...
But because it isn't *complete*.

You feel the space inside you — the space where something new could root.

You remember:
*I am not the wound.*
*I am not the mask.*
*I am not the coping.*

You are the one who endured…

And now, the one who decides.

The page turns.
The pen lands in your palm.
The story… is yours.

**A Sacred Invitation to Choose Your Path**

Cling to the Old Myth — It's familiar. It's safe. → Go to
Scene Two A below

Write the New One — Choose differently. Claim your voice.
→ Go to Scene Two B on page 105

Live Between Stories — Unsure. Undefined. In the void. →
Go to Scene Two C on page 106

---

## Scene Two A: The Re-Teller

You keep repeating the old story.
It's comfortable.
Predictable.

But your soul grows restless.
The myth wants to move.

Perhaps eventually… you'll say yes.

If you stay within the experience of narrative comfort, go to Path A at the end of this chapter, or…

If you're ready to re-examine the old plot, return to Chapter 1: The Fog Rolls In on page 7,

Or perhaps…

You hold a dusty book. The pages start rewriting themselves in your voice. If you feel inspired by the writing, leap to Chapter 16: The Trailhead on page 109.

---

## Scene Two B: The Author

You take the pen.
You write:
*I am…*
*I choose…*
*I remember…*

The story bends.

Not to erase what came before — but to re-weave it with truth.

If you stay within the experience of authorship, go to Path B at the end of this chapter, or…

If your identity is now sovereign, turn to Chapter 16: The Trailhead on page 109,

Or perhaps…

You find a scroll tucked in your pocket. It glows when you touch it. If you desire to read it, leap to Chapter 14: The Reclaiming on page 95.

---

## Scene Two C: The In-Between

You're in the void.
Not who you were.
Not yet who you're becoming.

It's tender.
It's true.
And it's necessary.

You learn to breathe in the in-between.
And trust that the myth is writing you, too.

If you stay within the experience of liminality, go to Path C at the end of this chapter, or…

If you're ready to name your truth, turn to Chapter 13: The Chamber of Treasures on page 89,

Or perhaps…

A blank page floats in the wind. If you chase it joyfully, leap to Chapter 16: The Trailhead on page 109.

# Chapter 15: Paths A, B, & C

---

**Path A** — You chose the old myth. And it will hold until you're ready to rewrite. The pen waits nearby.

From here, you may continue directly forward into Chapter 16: The Trailhead

---

**Path B** — You wrote your truth. You chose your myth. Now… you are ready to live it.

From here, you may continue directly forward into Chapter 16: The Trailhead

---

**Path C** — You lingered between identities. And that, too, is sacred ground. Even here… a new myth is unfolding.

From here, you may continue directly forward into Chapter 16: The Trailhead

# Chapter 16: The Trailhead

You now arrive at The Trailhead — the place where your story becomes a lived path. This is not the end. It is the turn of the spiral. A beginning disguised as an ending. A homecoming wrapped in mystery. Here, you stand not at a finish line, but at a threshold — carrying the medicine you gathered, the choices you made, the parts of yourself you reclaimed. The path is yours now. And it is alive. The invitation is to embrace your life fully with reverence, responsibility, joy, and radiant possibility.

**Opening Portal: Ritual Invitation**

The trail is not behind you — it begins beneath your feet. Consider one or more of the following ritual invitations:

• Trail Marker — Choose an object that represents this moment. Place it somewhere you'll see each day.

• 7-Day Anchor — Choose one new way of being, and live it for the next 7 days. Track what shifts.

• Voice it — Tell someone what you're embodying now. Let the words solidify your intention.

These rituals may return anytime you forget how far you've come.

## Scene One: The Beginning

It feels quiet.

Sacred.

Alive.

You're not the same version of you who began this book.

You're not who you'll become next.

You are here. A more awakened you. At the trailhead.

No map.

No manual.

Just a body that remembers.

A soul that says yes.

And a path that appears only as you walk it.

You realize: the teachings were never outside you.

They were always your own breath, your own bones, your own becoming.

The masks taught you protection.

The wounds taught you compassion.

The contracts taught you choice.

Grace taught you compassionate integrity.

Treasures taught you you were never empty.

Now, all that remains... is to live it.

**A Sacred Invitation to Choose Your Path**

Pause and Integrate — Let the journey settle. → Go to Scene Two A below

Surrender Fully — Begin living the new myth. → Go to Scene Two B on page 112

Feel Lost Again — Uncertainty returns. That's okay. → Go to Scene Two C on page 113

---

# Scene Two A: The Integrator

You don't rush.
You rest.
You let the journey land.

You know that embodiment doesn't come from speed — it comes from saturation.

You remember that integration is itself a sacred practice:
Stillness is medicine.
Ritual is medicine.
Silence is medicine.
Time is medicine.
Breath is medicine…

Todo es medicina.

You stay.

You listen.

You let the body lead.

If you stay within the experience of sacred integration, go to Path A at the end of this chapter, or...

A spiral forms in the sand. You walk it again — but differently now. Revisit any chapter whose medicine still calls.

---

## Scene Two B: The Embodied One

You say yes.
You choose again.
You live the new myth — not perfectly, but consciously.

You move with the tools you've reclaimed.
You speak the truths you once silenced.
You live in alignment, even when it's messy.

You become the walking prayer of your own becoming.
And you remember: embodiment is not about never forgetting — it is about remembering faster each time you do.

If you stay within the experience of sacred embodiment, go to Path B at the end of this chapter, or...

Invite others to witness your awakening. You are no longer alone. A new mountain rises in the distance. You bow to the

one you've just climbed. Revisit any chapter whose medicine
still calls.

---

## Scene Two C: The Wanderer

Doubt returns.
The fog drifts back.
And you wonder: did I really change?

Yes, beloved. You did.
Even if the mind forgets, the soul remembers.

This, too, is part of the journey.
The spiral does not erase uncertainty — it sanctifies it.

You recognize: feeling lost is proof you are still seeking. And
seeking is proof you are alive.

If you stay within the tender experience of uncertainty, go to
Path C at the end of this chapter, or...

A snake sheds its skin beside you. It nods as it disappears into
the forest. Return to Chapter 1: The Fog Rolls In — but read
it with new eyes.

## Chapter 16: Paths A, B, & C

**Path A** — You let it land. You took your time. And in that stillness, the path deepened.

**You are living the myth now.**

---

**Path B** — You rose everything from within you. Because everything you need is within you. You live aligned. You chose presence again and again.

**You are walking the myth now.**

---

**Path C** — You doubted. You forgot. But even then — you are still on the path.

**The myth is walking you now.**

## Closing Benediction

Beloved traveler, you have walked through the Chamber of Wounds. The first of the four chambers of the soul. The shadows faced, the pain given voice, and the first threads of wholeness returned. Every version of you is meant. You are complete in courage, vulnerability, love, and authenticity.

You also glimpsed the next three chambers: contracts, grace, and treasures. Go forward in tenderness...perhaps a further exploration of the chamber of contracts? The choice is, always and forever, yours.

www.ingramcontent.com/pod-product-compliance
Lightning Source LLC
Chambersburg PA
CBHW032049090426
42744CB00004B/142